Baby

Memory Book

First Year Memory Book
for Boys and Girls

This Book Belongs To:

Contents

1. Before You

Your Family Tree

About your Parents

Celebrating You

Pregnancy Milestones

2. You're Here

Birth Height, Weight, etc.

Your Feet and Hands

Current Events

3. You're Home

Your Nursery

4. Your Firsts

Life Experiences

First Holidays

5. You're Growing

Birthdays 1-11 months

Birthdays 2-5 years

BEFORE YOU

Family Tree

About Your Parents

NAME

BIRTHDAY

HOBBIES

FAVORITE MOVIE

FAVORITE SONG

About Your Parents

NAME

BIRTHDAY

HOBBIES

FAVORITE MOVIE

FAVORITE SONG

Celebrating You

picture
3.5"x2.5"

picture
3.5"x2.5"

picture
3.5"x2.5"

picture
3.5"x2.5"

Pregnancy Milestones

Due Date

Possible baby names

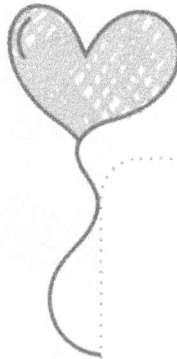

Sonogram picture
3.5"x2.5"

Best Reactions

Pregnancy Milestones

NOTES

YOU'RE HERE

PHOTO 5"x 3.5"

PHOTO 5"x 3.5"

PHOTO 5"x 3.5"

NAME

What it means

Why it was chosen

Height

Weight

TIME

FOOTPRINT

HANDPRINT

CURRENT EVENTS

CURRENT PRICES

NOTES

NOTES

Bringing You Home

Your Nursery

picture
3.5"x2.5"

picture
2.5"x3.5"

picture
2.5"x3.5"

picture
3.5"x2.5"

Bringing You Home
Your Nursery

DATE

_____

NOTES

_____

_____

_____

_____

_____

_____

_____

_____

_____

_____

First Outing

PICTURE
5"x3.5"

PICTURE
5"x3.5"

FIRST BATH

PICTURE
5"x3.5"

PICTURE
5"x3.5"

First Doctors Visit

PICTURE
3"x3.5"

PICTURE
3"x3.5"

First Baby Sitter

PICTURE
3"x3.5"

PICTURE
3"x3.5"

First Haircut

PICTURE
3"x3.5"

PICTURE
3"x3.5"

First Solid Food

PICTURE
3"x3.5"

PICTURE
3"x3.5"

First Easter

picture
2.5" x 3.5"

picture
3.5" x 2.5"

NOTES

picture
3.5" x 2.5"

First Valentines Day

picture
2.5" x 3.5"

picture
3.5" x 2.5"

love

NOTES

picture
3.5" x 2.5"

First 4th of July

picture
2.5" x 3.5"

picture
3.5" x 2.5"

NOTES

picture
3.5" x 2.5"

FIRST HALLOWEEN

picture
2.5" x 3.5"

picture
3.5" x 2.5"

NOTES

picture
3.5" x 2.5"

First Thanksgiving

picture
2.5" x 3.5"

picture
3.5" x 2.5"

NOTES

picture
3.5" x 2.5"

First Christmas

picture
2.5" x 3.5"

picture
3.5" x 2.5"

NOTES

picture
3.5" x 2.5"

First New Years

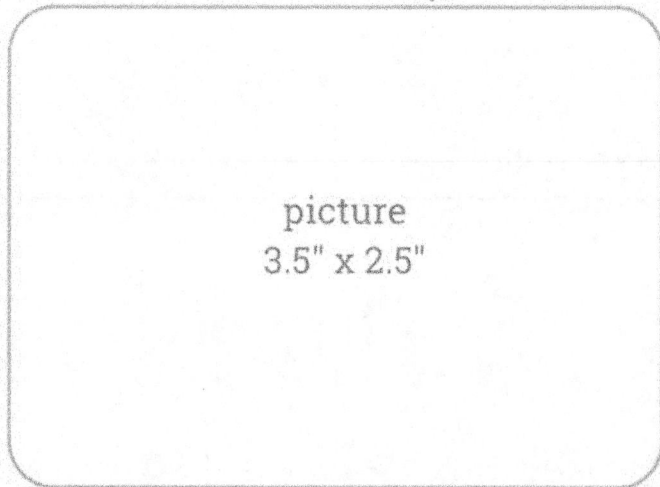

picture
2.5" x 3.5"

picture
3.5" x 2.5"

NOTES

picture
3.5" x 2.5"

Other Firsts

Other Firsts

1 Month Old

Height

Weight

Favorite toy

1 month old picture
3.5"x4"

Things You Like

Things You Disike

This Months Best Memory

2 Months Old

Height

Weight

Favorite toy

2 months old picture
3.5"x4"

Things You Like

Things You Disike

This Months Best Memory

3 Months Old

Height

Weight

Favorite toy

3 months old picture
3.5"x4"

Things You Like

Things You Disike

This Months Best Memory

4 Months Old

Height

Weight

Favorite toy

4 months old picture
3.5"x4"

Things You Like

Things You Disike

This Months Best Memory

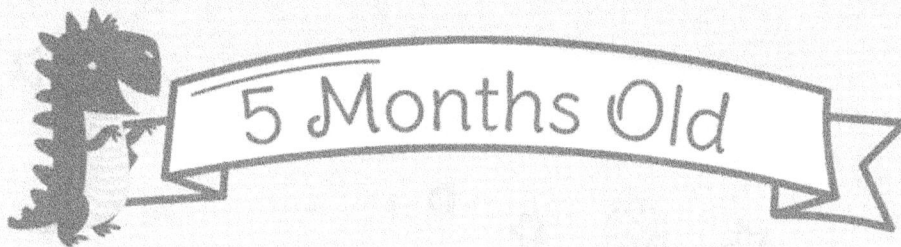

5 Months Old

Height

Weight

Favorite toy

5 months old picture
3.5"x4"

Things You Like

_____

_____

_____

Things You Disike

_____

_____

_____

This Months Best Memory

_____

_____

6 Months Old

Height

Weight

Favorite toy
_____

6 months old picture
3.5"x4"

Things You Like
_____
_____
_____

Things You Disike
_____
_____
_____

This Months Best Memory
_____
_____

7 Months Old

Height

Weight

Favorite toy

7 months old picture
3.5"x4"

Things You Like

Things You Disike

This Months Best Memory

8 Months Old

Height

Weight

Favorite toy

8 months old picture
3.5"x4"

Things You Like

Things You Disike

This Months Best Memory

9 Months Old

Height

Weight

Favorite toy

9 months old picture
3.5"x4"

Things You Like

Things You Disike

This Months Best Memory

10 Months Old

Height

Weight

Favorite toy

10 months old picture
3.5"x4"

Things You Like

Things You Dislike

This Months Best Memory

11 Months Old

Height

Weight

Favorite toy

11 months old picture
3.5"x4"

Things You Like

Things You Disike

This Months Best Memory

Your First Birthday!

picture
2" x 2.5"

picture
2.5" x 3.5"

picture
2" x 2.5"

picture
3" x 2.5"

picture
3" x 2.5"

Your First Birthday!

Height and Weight

Vocabulary

Favorite gifts

How we celebrated

2 Years Old

picture
2" x 2.5"

picture
2.5" x 3.5"

picture
2" x 2.5"

picture
3" x 2.5"

picture
3" x 2.5"

2 Years Old

Your Art

Height

Best memories from the last year

Favorite gifts

3 Years Old

Your Art

Height

Best memories from the last year

Favorite gifts

3 Years Old

picture
2" x 2.5"

picture
2.5" x 3.5"

picture
2" x 2.5"

picture
3" x 2.5"

picture
3" x 2.5"

4 Years Old

picture
2" x 2.5"

picture
2.5" x 3.5"

picture
2" x 2.5"

picture
3" x 2.5"

picture
3" x 2.5"

4 Years Old

Your Art

Height

Best memories from the last year

Favorite gifts

5 Years Old

picture
2" x 2.5"

picture
2.5" x 3.5"

picture
2" x 2.5"

picture
3" x 2.5"

picture
3" x 2.5"

5 Years Old

Your Art

Height

Best memories from the last year

Favorite gifts

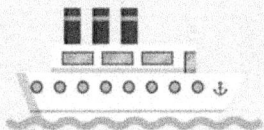
OUR TRAVELS

NOTES

picture 4.5"x3.5"

picture 2.5"x3.5"

picture 3.5"x2.5"

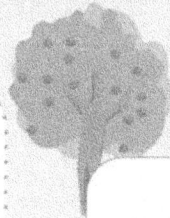

picture 4.5"x3.5"

picture 3.5"x2.5"

picture 2.5"x3.5"

picture 4.5"x3.5"

picture 2.5"x3.5"

picture 3.5"x2.5"

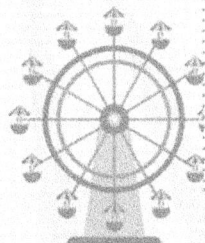

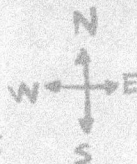

picture 4.5"x3.5"

picture 3.5"x2.5"

picture 2.5"x3.5"

picture 4.5"x3.5"

picture 3.5"x2.5"

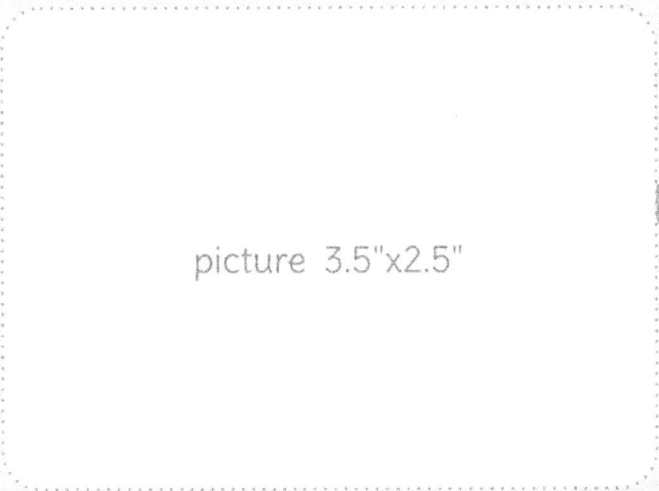

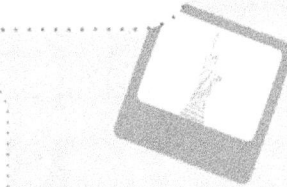

picture 2.5"x3.5"

picture 4.5"x3.5"

picture 3.5"x2.5"

picture 2.5"x3.5"

NOTES

NOTES

NOTES

NOTES

NOTES

NOTES

NOTES

NOTES

NOTES

NOTES

NOTES

NOTES

www.ingramcontent.com/pod-product-compliance
Lightning Source LLC
LaVergne TN
LVHW061249060426
835508LV00018B/1555

9781948802581